TALKING TO STRANGERS:

Poetry of Everyday Life

By Peter Neil Carroll

TALKING TO STRANGERS:

Poetry of Everyday Life

By Peter Neil Carroll

First Edition

Published by Turning Point Books
P.O. Box 541106
Cincinnati, OH 45254-1106
www.turningpointbooks.com

Manufactured in the USA.

Cover photograph: *Bar*, Jeannette Ferrary, ©2020

Designed by Debra Turner

Library of Congress Cataloging-in-Publication Data
Peter Neil Carroll

Talking to Strangers: Poetry of Everyday Life
ISBN: 9781625493989

For Jeannette

"I was so poorly formed,
  never able to learn a thing,
  and if I didn't bark it is because back then
  they did not teach me to bark."

— Pablo Neruda
"The Natural Gentleman"

"Can anything good come out
of the Bronx, driving a green Buick."

— Andrea Hinding (1971)

ACKNOWLEDGMENTS

Thanks to the many editors who first published these poems, some with revisions.

Arkansas Review: "Making Peace"

Amsterdam Quarterly: "The Americans"

BigCityLit: "Talking to Strangers"

Cultural Weekly: "Hitchhiker"

Fresh Water Poetry Review: "Swept Away"

Marin Poetry Anthology, 2021: "The Table" (Orig. title "A Case of Identity Correction")

Portside.org: "Unreliable Narrator"; "Wall Street Occupied"

Thanks

Poetry is not such a lonely enterprise as some may think. More and more it becomes a community affair. My Saturday Morning poets continue to inspire and nourish me: Terry Adams, Mary Bailey, Anne Chelek, Esther Kamkar, Lisa Rizzo, Lee Rossi and Brenda Simmons know how to keep a poet honest. Friends like Lee and Charlotte Muse generously offered comments and suggestions of this emerging manuscript. I also thank my hosts at various readings for the opportunity to test my voice aloud: Patrick Daly and Charlotte Muse of the Not Yet Dead Poets in Redwood City; Kathleen Beasley and Jacki Rigoni of my hometown Belmont Library; the usual crowd at San Jose's Willow Glen Library; Peter Stansky who hosts the Company of Authors series at Stanford and is always a treat to be part of; Andrew Lee at the Puffin Foundation series in Teaneck, New Jersey; Gary Jones at the American International College in Springfield, Massachusetts; Ramon & Judy Sender of San Francisco's Odd Monday Series; Sandra Anfang of the Rivertown poets in Petaluma; Jenna Varden of the San Mateo Public Library; Anne Huang of the Traveling Show of the Marin Poetry Center; and Diane Moomey and Steve Long of Café Society in Half Moon Bay. Much delight, too, for this book's appearance goes to Debra Turner of dtDesign. Turning Point's Kevin Walzer and Lori Jareo have once again been a pleasure to work with. And none of this would matter without the love I share with Jeannette Ferrary.

Contents

PART 4

PART 5

PART 6

PART 7

PART 1

Talking to Strangers

I like talking to strangers when I travel
though limit my curiosity to chit-chat,
so yesterday on the plane to New York
I noticed a light-haired flight attendant
whose Irish face reminded me
of Caroline Kennedy. I asked
in a friendly way if she was leaving home
or heading home. She stammered for a moment,
frowned, trying hard to reply.
It occurred to me that Caroline K might not
be as happy as she looks in magazines either.
After we landed, I squeezed into a rush-hour
subway, everyone bulked with coats
and backpacks but a nice Caribbean woman
swiveled around so I could reach a pole
before the train jerked ahead. We stood
smiling with our eyes, the cars lumbering
until I felt a jolt and the train stopped—
tossing us together in a tunnel, lights
flickering, the motor dead. I thought
we shouldn't be meeting like this, and said
it aloud. Stuck for twenty minutes, she had time
to tell me about her children, two grown
and gone, the youngest 13, who, she said,
is obsessed with her hair but she'll get over it.
Yes, I agreed, just as the man behind me spoke
from a shadow, recommending the woman try
a new conditioner he's using, prompting
another voice in the dark to tout a hair salon,
leading yet another passenger to google its address.
Free advice running rampant underground,
we'd created a community. When the train
finally reached a station, I straggled off, realizing
no one had mentioned God's blessings,
the Creator of the Universe no doubt weary
of heavenly shampoos. All this chatter
left me wondering if Caroline K has begun
to color her hair, she's nobody's child any more.

4 PM in a DC Bar

This is my last fling, she says.
I'm going back to Houston
tomorrow. I used to work in
this place. I was a cashier
until a half hour ago. I hate
that fucking bullshit boss.
So I'm going back to Houston
tomorrow afternoon. I'm
going to get up early and walk
around the streets and then
I'm going back to Houston.

No man, I don't want a drink.
I'm not polite, it's not that.
I'm spaced out from this
crazy day. I'm so spaced
that I can't drink a thing.
I'm not meaning to be
unsociable but I'm going
to have some black coffee.

He always bullshits women,
that shit. He's creepy putting
his hands all over me. And
after I told him to keep his
bullshitting hands to himself,
he hates me. The crazy shit.
I thought I'd get him a girl
friend so he'd leave me alone.
But none of my friends would
go near him. It's no wonder.

What can he expect, the shit.
I'm an American, you know.
I was born in this country.
In Texas.

Hitchhiker

Dawn, driving through Jersey suburbs, I see
a thumb wagging, brake fast, taking her in—
light hair, tight jeans, lots of mascara.

Stop here, she orders in half-a-mile, pointing
to a solitary Chevy parked at a littered curb.
Someone, she claims, has stolen her purse.

Doors unlocked, I search for the keys, find
none. The trunk is sealed. Neither locksmith
nor felon, I can't retrieve her precious cargo.

Though helpless, she's not distraught, rather
calmly asks if I'd drive her home. A poker term
comes to mind: in for a nickel, in for a dime,

but first she reaches into the back seat, saying
you might as well take it, offers my reward—
a gallon container of peanut oil. Can I refuse?

Entering the city, I break silence, ask her what
she does. *Dancer.* And I guess that's why she's
up early with so much makeup. Where, I wonder.

She names a well-known strip club, tourist bait.
I'm stuck for a response, decide not to question
her dance style, but inquire about the clientele.

Mostly married guys, she says, lonely guys, losers.
I'm surprised. My thoughts turn to my lucky self.
Just lookers, she adds. They're not allowed to touch.

Here, she announces, in front of a redbrick row house
on a tree-lined street, *My halfway house*—and leaves
me to ponder what to do with all that peanut oil.

How Little We Knew

My son, facing a mid-life birthday, asks
why his middle name is Douglas. Why not?
No one else I knew needed to be named after,

but news came on a gray Sunday in January,
Chicago's hawk-wind blowing misery
off the lake. A man driving a Volkswagen

on a neon-stained night had braked too late.
We gathered in my flat to remember David,
a graduate student, how little of him

we knew, anecdotes, nothing of the accident.
His father was a professor, we didn't know
of what. We were young men, a few women

(no children yet) but David looked older,
graying, soft-spoken with Midwest irony.
How best to show our respect, our grief?

Let's make a scholarship fund, someone said,
though we were too poor to fund ourselves.
Later, we'd say his name, clink glasses, shake

heads, wonder how his girlfriend was doing.
Someone said they were about to split up.
Nothing was certain. When my wife became

pregnant we honored David in our son's middle
initial, D, a small gesture. Better than nothing.

Strangers on a Plane

Because the man in 5B,
hearing the pilot announce
our destination, raced
through the front exit,

I learn from his discarded
newspaper the life
& hard times of
Howard "Knot" Smith,

late of Cairo, Illinois,
U.S. Marine Corps veteran
Pacific Theater of Operations,
member of Veterans

of Foreign Wars and the
First Baptist Church,
worked hard, never married.
Knot was an avid dancer.

Arrival

Coming out of Penn Station, it's a frigid walk
to the funky Tick Tock diner on Eighth and 34TH,
already smoky from fried eggs, scorched coffee.

I slide into a booth near a European couple taking
breakfast photos, plates piled with syrupy waffles,
sweet rolls, soft eggs, enough to feed a barracks,
so much abundance flows from America's hearth.

Glancing through the window, I see a ragged man
jaywalk to a curbside trash bin, shuffling newspapers
as if looking for something to read but instead snaps
open a lighter, ignites the paper and takes off running.

Yellow flames rise, but reduce to a smoldering fire.
Many people walk past the burning bin, some not
noticing at all, some admire the latest miracle on 34TH
Street but no one rings an alarm or summons help.

At last, a loud rumble outside, a fire engine jolts to a stop,
two firefighters (man and woman) in rubber uniforms leap
out, study the smoky bin, poke the ashes, the flames
come to life. They douse the blaze with white liquid.

At the corner, a wind-burned man sits on cardboard,
he's been watching the show. Before leaving, I buy coffee,
loaded with cream and sugar, pay a visit to the guy sitting
on the sidewalk. You OK? He accepts my gift without thanks,
grunts, takes a sip, stirs some phlegm, hawks into the gutter.

Samaritans

8TH Avenue, #421, here's the stalwart U.S. Post Office
where my father sorted mail after the Army. Today an army
of homeless huddles under blankets and coats on the cold
concrete steps. The sky gray, flurries signal worse to come.

A steamy smell from a deli draws me inside, I sit next
to a man dressed in a suit, white shirt, tie, his eyes blood-
shot. First thing he says, *I'm sick,* and sticks his hand
into a brown paper bag, half-hiding a green bottle.

When the liquid reaches his lips, he chokes, spits, douses
the counter. *I'm sorry,* he apologizes. *It's only 14 percent.*
What can I say? It doesn't matter what I say. He's thirsty.
It's that simple. *Get me to a rehab, he asks. I need help.*

I go to wash my hands, return to see him outside, the pint
in his fist, his eyes jittery. *They threw me out,* he says. I ask
where he wants to go, get an address, hail a taxi, pay the fare.
He waves bye-bye from the backseat as they pull into traffic.

Samaritans are patrolling sidewalks and crannies, urging
the homeless to move indoors. One guy sits, bare feet at the curb,
head against a hydrant, lost in dreams, while a man in a navy cap
tugs gently on his torn tweed coat, hugging him to his feet.

The man without a home looks back, eyes pleading for escape.

Wind Chill

The bitter outside keeps the place still,
just one fellow two stools down minding
his business, a young couple at a corner
candle-lit table, speaking softly.

Two Scotches, I make a trip to the john
and when I return, tuxedoed waiters are
singing *Happy Birthday, Dear Donna.*
She shuts her eyes, blows out candles.

I slip onto my stool, the lone man turns,
announces loudly, *You missed the toast.*
I had to pee, I explain. He gets the point,
slides his highball down the bar closer.

He has friends, he goes on, two brothers,
having a contest about who can pee on
the most national monuments. They're over
a hundred. He orders us another round.

I'm from North Dakota, he says—*Ever been?*
Five winters, I blurt, knowing in one minute
he'll be talking Winter, not something folks
treat lightly even in July. You had to be ready.

Storm windows, furnaces, snow tires, tune-ups:
we talk blizzards and ice, guys driving into
drifts, falling off frozen roofs, finding stiffs
in the morning. I had to leave to stay alive.

My new friend breathes whiskey, smirks, says
with jealous eyes, *So you're a goddam quitter!*
Look who's talking, I think (but do not say)
two geezers sitting cozy in a New York bar.

The Prophet

Homebound commuters stuffed in quilted coats,
scarves, gloves, skull caps, boots, staring in space,
doze on subway seats when a heavy voice booms

Look out! demanding passengers make way. Give a damn,
please… fragments I hear…*that damned president…*
God won't forgive… Another crank in underground Gotham

approaches, but before I see him, a woolly dog arrives,
harnessed in leather, a guide dog, then the bulky man,
eyes wide open, milky blue, sightless, cursing sinners,

nameless politicians, warning God's wrath will punish
this carload of witnesses. Struck dumb by his rage, no one
replies or moves, except to clear a path for the lop-sided dog.

A dark woman makes eye contact, silently we worry, timid
spectators assessing some vague threat or further announcement,
perhaps a common fate, a state of patient alertness, ready for

what may or not happen as the train lurches to a station.
The doors grumble open, the dog leads the way out, the pair
wobble on the platform. We strangers, relieved that nothing

dire has occurred, follow outside, watch them enter the next car.
The doors shut. The story's over. We pause another moment,
looking for a word. She turns away first, I wait a second, separate.

I'm left to wonder what the Prophet wanted us to do, besides
measure our distance, note his bitter presence this winter day.
Outside, silence captures the city, stoplights changing colors—

green glare, red glare—30-second turns except when police cars
crawl up deserted streets, lights flaring. And then the snowfall
abruptly stops, the sky blackens, crystal stars begin to speak.

The Gift

Thomas sits near the window
on the far side of the classroom.
We are six. He is not
the only confused child but
the boy who one day refuses
to leave his desk at lunchtime.

Our teacher, red-faced, pulls
on his long arm, wrenching,
dragging him off his seat,
his body collapses on the chalky-
dust floor. Her rage frightens
us all into silence.

Thomas seldom utters a word
even when we read aloud,
the storybook titled Times & Places.
I guess Thomas has no place,
no lunch to go home to.

The class lines up by size, speeds
downstairs, races for home. My mother,
as she does every day, toasts
a bacon and tomato sandwich,
pours a glass of cold milk.

Thomas doesn't return the next day
or ever, but a year later
my parents purchase a "love seat,"
invite a man and wife to adopt
our old couch. While adults
wrestle with furniture, I notice
Thomas waiting at the landing.

Without a moment's thought, I grab
my stack of Superman comics, give
them all to Thomas. His eyes shine
at the windfall before he turns
away without a word.

PART 2

Ward Avenue, The Bronx

I'm first out in the morning, street asleep
except for the very old pair looking out their window—
he rabbinical, gray-bearded, she with quivering lips—
unwelcoming the disturbance.

I bounce a pink ball against the stoop,
catch the rebound but already
the old man's long-arm gesture
shoos me away.

Maybe another boy will come out to play.

Few dogs roam the street but at least three of mixed breed
are named Lucky, maybe because they live charmed lives,
maybe they are fetishes, protecting those who feed them.

All I want is a fire station dog named Spots.

There's Sandy, a woolly-haired beast shaped like a pig
that sleeps winter and summer on the sidewalk in the sun.

No one I know keeps a cat.

Every afternoon after lunch a thin man in a faded army
uniform, watery blue eyes staring far ahead, strides
behind two Irish setters on leather leashes until they near
the empty lots. He releases them to race away.

A little later the three return to the soldier's parked car,
he's left his son Joey locked inside. All the while his wife
works in a laundry folding sheets and towels.

More than once Joey comes to my door, begging
my mother to let him in so he can kiss me.

She never does.

Running Bases

We loitered, we darted, we hid
behind fenders of parked cars,
under axles reeking of grease.

The skill of matadors we learned,
dodging manic drivers, enormous
gear-grinding trucks, risky

on everyday walks—to school,
to the candy store, to watch
a neighbor's TV,

especially the hazardous game,
running bases, each score
a race curb to curb.

And distance, what is distance
to the eye of a child,
how far away is safe?

I saw boys bounced on cement,
and once the shadow of a body,
a kid named Michael or David,

blood in a gutter, blotted
by newspaper. How closely
the mothers watched us that day.

Swept Away

The sound of a broom knocking
against the legs of kitchen chairs, what
my mother did most mornings after
my big sister went to school,
my father off to teach eighth graders
music appreciation, and I, just
starting kindergarten would rush
to the piano to bang away with two hands
some symphonic chaos I thought would
prepare me for work in later life, as it
had for my father, but was interrupted
by my mother's vacuum cleaner
drowning out my performance. I'd
run to the window to watch other men
getting their cars to go to work, as
I expected to do some day. Later
I held my mother's hand as she led
me to school, passing a neighbor girl,
Marjorie, a few weeks younger than I,
sadly ineligible for kindergarten
who begged me not to go to school
but stay and play with her, a distressed
plea I dismissed, saying, *I need to go.*
Do you want your husband to be stupid?

Rules

There were strict rules in those days.
No children allowed but everything
I learned about rules I learned from
my father, the art of disobedience.

Startled when he pulls down the iron
fire escape—what is he thinking?—
no time to be afraid, I follow his feet
up the shaky ladder, keep my eyes

on the metal handrail and black steps
as he instructed, though once around
the fifth floor I chance to look down
at the faraway ground, feeling dizzy

until we reach the seventh floor where
my mother recuperates from surgery.
He helps me crawl through an open
curtained window, pulls me to my feet.

I was 7 and see now it was an errand
of mercy. My mother had been there
for a week. I'd sent a get-well card
and she'd replied in scrawl on a pad.

My mother rouses from half-sleep.
I notice tubes taped to her arm,
afraid to approach too closely, but
too soon Big Nurse enters, glaring.

There's a child here! she barks. Quickly,
as we ride the elevator down, my father
reminds me, all they can do is throw us
out, and off we went for chocolate malts.

Pride has its own reward: this mix of
courage and stupidity. My mother was
furious when she learned what we did,
and I never climbed a fire escape again.

Misplaced Person

There were no sidewalks in Queens
only flat dirt paths that softened
into puddles amid melting snow.

That first spring day I lost my grounding—
the hard, concrete turf of the city.
My feet squished, my knees buckled.

The local boys were accustomed to muck,
braver, wilder than my old gang, diving
into open foundations, robbing stores.

Mickey, the bully, was the most graceful
athlete. Frank the best liar, Ralph shyest,
Billy Hardluck most likely to fumble.

The newest kid, I was the one who couldn't
ride a two-wheeler, who liked to read,
who flinched at the pop of an air rifle.

Uprooted, I never overcame a sense
of unbelonging, a condition I did not
choose and did not mind.

Mario

Everyone in the neighborhood knew Mario,
the man in a wheelchair, a poor immigrant
seized by paralysis who managed with his
own hands to build a room and a ramp,
his only assistance from two young sons.

Local news celebrated the achievement. Mario
then learned to make hand-wrought jewelry—
rings, bracelets, crucifixes for children of all faiths.
Mothers bought his Christmas and Easter gifts.
Tears ran when he described his divine blessing.

His passion remained in concrete—that is to say,
supervising the boys as they hammered frames,
laid sidewalks, a patio, put up a "wishing well."
One summer, he decided to erect a holy shrine,
set the boys to work to teach them his skills.

They were barely teenagers. When they stumbled
in their labor, Mario's piety turned to rage.
Hard heads, he screamed in Italian, knocking
their skulls with a long-handled hoe. You could
see their enlarged muscles clench in fear.

Every weekend they went to church for Confession.
In high school they hung with tough hoods, swaggered
and spat, went home like lambs. At 18, they took off
forever. Mario never complains. He prays quietly
in his chair, sometimes plays tunes on an accordion.

On the Death of Whitey Ford

The great itch began the day my eight-year old friend Alec Slowball,
told me pitcher Whitey Ford was joining the Yankees next season.
I'd never heard of Whitey Ford, but now he was out of the Army.
He became my star. I learned to throw sliders, curves, knuckleballs.

Big deal, but of no use, until a pack of old wolves began to gather
in the school yard Sunday mornings, big men in their 30s, 40s,
truck drivers, cabbies, whites and blacks, a Chinese, one parole officer,
all past their prime, but eager to capture a few hours of lost youth.

Center fielder Big Robbie opened coke bottles with his teeth. Catcher
Cliff, a cross-eyed barman, wore glasses under the mask. The Chinese
outfielder was ambidextrous. Taxi Max limped from his war wounds.
Little Robbie ran like a rabbit until a wild pitch blasted his kidneys.

One day, they were a man short. I got my chance, managed two bunts
and two strike outs, but on the last play, I caught the ball in deep right
field and sent a telegram to Cliff, who tagged out the runner, winning
the game. I got plenty of arm bumps, felt like a hero. I was fourteen.

The next week, I went to the field early, throwing warmups, hoping
to get into the game. Taxi Max did a head count, handed me a paper
cup of coffee. I was a made man, sipping my first taste of adult life.
I played with them all summer, though I never got better at bat.

Whitey Ford went on to glory, Mickey Mantle drank himself into a grave,
Alec Slowball became a gym teacher. Those vets who let me play dropped
away one by one, as did I. For years, I struggled to write a novel about
the man with a bad foot, a kid with an electric arm. Now, I'm a poet.

Dottie

She had a sense of humor.
Mother of my friend Frank,
his twin sisters, she named
their bony white-tailed
female dog *Dagmar* after
a voluptuous TV actress.

Red-haired colleen,
she told jokes that ended
with a wink, took a turn
swinging a bat in short shorts.
I liked the way she moved.

I see her sitting on the top
step of the stoop wearing
a royal blue blouse that had
lost a strategic button and
a black brassiere. All the boys
noticed, even shy Ralph
who whispered,
I like the way she dresses.

We were 13, at the verge
of things we didn't know.
To be fair, she wasn't exactly
seductive, but it didn't take much
at our age to exaggerate.

Now lured by delayed fantasy,
I track her down, find both her girls
had daughters, both had recently died,
but Dottie is alive, kicking at 96,
describes herself *Single*. And what
now can an old boy say
that she would want to hear?

The Tailor's Tale

June, month of proms, weddings, rented
tuxedos, the season affluent parents send
children to summer camp, which means
name tags sewn on shorts, shirts, socks.

Irwin the haberdasher assures his tailor—me—
that no one will notice if I make mistakes,
gives me lessons on how to lie to customers
about trouser lengths, affixing the names.

One day, business slow (non-existent), he
invites me into his bare office, lights a cigar,
starts telling me war stories, his interviews
with ex-Nazis. Everyone claimed innocence.

Truth is not Irwin's strong suit these days
since he's having an affair with a blonde
who arrives every Tuesday afternoon.
He sends me home early, locks the door,

One Wednesday, his wife shows up, eyeing
the dressing room, informs "Stupid Irwin"
that her father, who set him up in this racket,
will kill his line of credit. I fear for my pay.

Next day, as I treadle the old sewing machine,
he sends me off to deliver a sealed envelope
to a divorce lawyer in Brooklyn. His prospects
certainly do not look like good news.

Later, he corners me in his office, red-eyed but
guilty. *I wasn't always such a fuck up,* he says.
He slips me a five-dollar bill, which is how I lost
my job— padlocked doors, names on the floor.

Morning Line

Before hitting the ugly streets at dawn,
we young mailmen would pause at the pitted counter
of Rob's diner, hands wrapped on steaming cups,
read the morning line on the evening's harness races
and mope about the latest speedups concocted by
our new supervisor (Jake the Snake), all the while
half staring at a large chunk of pound cake that sat
untouched in its plastic case most of the summer—
only once in twelve weeks did its shape change
when someone decided a big slice might hit the spot—
and that once changed our whole view of the job.

What fool? What idiot? someone shouted into
the smoky haze. *Call out the Board of Health!*
One among us had secretly torn off a piece, left it
to pass hand to hand as if it came from mama's kitchen.
Amazement, then waves of laughter percolated
the room like gurgling pots, we laughed like maniacs;
days afterward mere eye contact, an upturned nose,
brought out the rare camaraderie of survivors,
blessed as the lucky ones who'd missed the Titanic,
what personal miracle had spared us ptomaine,
as if a secret handshake had given secret wisdom.
In ten minutes, as we faced the ugly streets again,
cocksure, we could take anything the bastards put out.

The Professor

For John J. McDermott (1932-2018)
". . .no second acts in American lives."
—F. Scott Fitzgerald

Passing a classroom one day, I heard a man shout,
saw him grinding chalk on a blackboard and met
the great philosophy professor who woke me up.
He taught like an evangelical—*Ideas matter!*

And when I spoke to him twenty years later the man
who changed my life was a mess. His wife had left,
his kids conspired to have him arrested. Fresh from
the drunk tank, his voice was shaky, raw, tense.

He called me his bookends, one who knew him only
before and after the bad times, when he lived on quarts
of vodka. He found some relief reciting how low he had
fallen, the miracle of a survival that left him stricken.

He'd glimpsed how close he came to zero when he tripped
on a curb and a policeman kicked his ass. Years on the bum
taught him of chemical linkage, body and soul, how genius
was forced to its knees, and he would always live with pain.

He never left the classroom, never gave a lecture twice, taught
two more generations why ideas do matter. He's dead one year—
old age, natural causes—but stays alive in one word: Teacher.
Every class became an opportunity, he exulted in the third act.

Strangers of Brooklyn

I met her years ago, a poet exiled in Minnesota,
reminiscing about her Brooklyn childhood,

trauma implied, how she carefully undressed
her dolls *so they would never hurt me,*

the time big Frankie Clifford pushed her sled
down an icy driveway, warning, *Don't forget*

to steer (but she never knew how to steer),
a knee-scar proving the narrow escape.

She returns, a stranger now, measures memory
against fact, that driveway merely five-feet long

lacks the slightest slope of peril. She tells me
how little has changed, the house, that is,

the second-story window framing her view
of the world from her pink bedroom.

How different look the residents, whites replaced,
new folks, darker people, improving the old turf.

Those "newcomers," here now two generations
as wary as these visitors, wonder

Who are these whites? maybe real estate agents
or cops looking for trouble?

But after I confide to a curious Caribbean woman,
our mission of nostalgia, her eyes brighten.

Nothing to fear, she repeats my story to another
neighbor. All's right for a long walk.

My poet friend rises on her toes, stymied by a high
slatted fence hiding the backyard, remembers gardens

lined with brick paths, with roses, with kitchen herbs.
She pictures what it looked like but refuses to confirm it.

Knock on the door, I plead. *They'll welcome you.*
But she won't. She just won't.

Coney Blues

Our losses are endless, Coney Island
proves that none of us is brave enough

to ride the Cyclone rollercoaster,
or dare a parachute jump.

It's safer on the windy boardwalk
watching muscle men lift great weights

and skinny pre-pubescent girls performing
splits backwards, upside down.

We breathe deeply salt-sea winds, hear the squawk
of gulls, the rumble of ocean

and, yes, we are grown old.

PART 3

Crossing from Brooklyn

*And you that shall cross from shore to shore
years hence are more to me...than you might suppose.*
—Leaves of Grass

September afternoon, the air crisp,
a steady wind from the west drags
distant clouds closer, pushing gulls away.
A taxi helicopter ratchets and grinds.

I stop midway at the rail, watch the river
running fast, tugboats climbing white caps,
the wake of a ferry, a lone sailor in a canoe,
two shirtless boys competing on jet skis.

So many lovers' scribbles: Seb + Steph,
Vetlana + Valera, Marco & Celine—
and tens of thousands more writ but
erased each rainfall, each blizzard.

Many grifters, too—a bearded man drags
a twelve-foot yellow snake to frighten girls
or charm them. A lady in black sells pencils,
keychains, a thin book of Brooklyn verse.

Add another million selfies, lovers grinning.
But no cynicism, please. The sun is real,
the air suffused with Atlantic salt, great
skylines: buildings shining on both shores.

The antique bridge still arouses desire,
temptation, what graffiti artists
repeat as I tread over the iron span:
Live Your Dreams; Dream Your Life!

The North River

Tugs and barges, ferries to Jersey, speedboats and sails,
at a rail I stop to watch fast-running traffic, and a voice

behind me calls, *Nice day.* I turn, a bearded gent sits alone,
eating an egg sandwich out of a paper bag. Nice, I agree.

Be-au-ti-ful, he says stretching the word. *I come every week
to watch the waters mixing.* He points to the Narrows, the big

river opening to Atlantic seas. *That's the magic spot where
the water touches the sky,* he says. A kindred spirit I've found.

He's a talker too, introduces himself, Lou, lives on Long Island,
says he doesn't need a house by the water. *I come here for free.*

He's excited for what he can never own—the river, the boats,
the sun. *I come to get away from my life. You know what I mean?*

Lou's long story—the military, a divorce, daughters not speaking
to him, never sees his grandkids. The river hears his loneliness.

Rain and No Rain

Good day for ducks, stopping under storefront
awnings, overhangs, I make my way up 1st Avenue
to Spanish Harlem where my dad grew up, a street
on a hill that sloped toward the East River.

Two police boats cruise the shoreline, disappear
under the shadow of the Queensboro Bridge.
Briefly I shelter under its cover near a woman
with frizzy red hair holding a red-haired Pekinese.

A crack of thunder sends me into a 24-hour diner
imprecisely named The Palace, its menu the size
of a small-city phone book, food from all nations.
I pick patriotic grilled American cheese, pickle,

and apple pie. *Just like my mother made,* I quip
to the weary waiter, who snaps a New York answer,
Even mothers, believe me, they didn't do it so good.
Which may be the truth.

Another cup of coffee delays entering wet streets,
Spanish Harlem is now off the radar. When it lets up,
I hasten to the subway only to find rain has flooded
the tracks, all trains running late.

When I ask a Hispanic crewman his forecast, he looks
behind before answering. *Bad work. Too fast. Not careful.
Like always. Look,* he points to glazed-tiles from which
water is now dripping into a pool. *Believe it or not.*

Doors of Perception

A noon shower chases me
into THINK café, named probably
for student patrons, most busy
on Facebook, playing games or asleep.

Here I'm an anachronism,
dragging a second-hand book,
Aldous Huxley's *Doors of Perception*,
memoir of a 1950s chemistry experiment
tracing effects of mescaline.

As Huxley says:
The mescaline taker sees no reason
to do anything in particular
because he has
better things to think about.

Which leads me to notice
the lack of books in THINK
just as a woman at the next table
raises her eye, asks
Why are you reading that?

She's wearing a large
blue-green floral tattoo
that disappears up her silk sleeve,
discreet exhibitionism
that intrigues me.

Good question I answer,
have you read it? Nope, but says
she's a grad student, she's heard of Huxley.
Cool, I reply. She glances at
the plain yellow cover. *Is it good?*

Dated, I reply. She stares for a moment,
returns to her screen.
Me, too. I'm dated, done.
So I head for the real door,
perceive the sun is still here,
and take another walk
around Washington Square.

On the High-Line

A week of clouds, the eye craves sunlight,
I climb a column of metal stairs to
the elevated High-Line, an unused railway
perched above the Hudson River, sky bright,
excellent views of the waterfront, the old city.

Thousands of world travelers (seldom natives)
parade along the defunct spur line, buried
in winter under frozen weeds, dirty snow.

What would Piet Minuit think?— he of the $24
grand theft of the island—or the lackeys
of the Duke of York? I know more about
the planet Mars than they knew
about Henry Hudson's river.

Tourists marvel at flim-flam architecture, brick
walls spray-painted with slogans. Whitewash
refreshes the backside of buildings, fire escapes
scraped of rust, acres crumble, replaced by plank.

Artists install black glass, chrome, angled walls.
In this age of cell snapshots, every witness wants
a selfie, proof of their presence. A woman in green
wool turns to study an exceptional zebra design.

A man calls loudly, *Mary, look at me!* She swivels,
pre-formed smile, he clicks, reminding her
she's not on holiday to sight-see,
the city only a backdrop for future memory.

Stopping at a bench, I hear a young girl complain, her
foot sore. *I'll rub it for you* her dad replies, unbuckling
a soft-soled slipper, Chinese embroidery, bare comfort
on concrete. So much culture resides in footwear.

Germans stride in high-back leather or boots; the English
waddle in light-weight trainers; a French woman stops to
rest, slides off a long-pointed red leather toe. The American,
me, looks down, discovers a hole in my shoe, cracked at the heel.

I want to ask the girl's father to rub my foot, but before I can,
he lifts her to his shoulder, kisses her cheek, moves on.

Oral Tradition

Coming down the High-Line at 34TH Street, I pass
through a crowd of construction workers eating lunch
and see a small pantomime playing out on a street
between a pair of traffic police in uniforms,

white officer's caps and bright smocks—the man's is
orange, the woman's shiny chartreuse, so they're seen
easily by speeding traffic. She is brown-skinned, wears
blonde dreadlocks that spill under her cap. He's older,

a white ethnic, holds a white pennant, moving it through
the air to explain a proper motion, she with an orange
pennant copies his moves. His knees bend as he waves
a hand and she's an apt student learning the tricks.

That's the tip for the day, he says as I approach them,
an oral tradition passing smoothly through the ranks.

Surveillance

Most mornings a crowd of tourists climbs the ramp to
the High-Line, offering clear views of the westside river.
but today I'm distracted by strange activity in a parking lot.

Hand signals, backups, drivers hopping in and out, padlocked
doors, constant cargo inspections. A man steps from a shack
leading a shaggy yellow dog to a van, then to the rear trunk.

The mutt appears satisfied, everything in order. The men chat,
the dog wobbles to his shade. Doors shut, the truck exits to
a side street, stops at a light, gets lost in traffic.

The line of vans moves forward, inspections continue, carpets,
boxes of shelving, who knows what, the men chat, the yellow dog
does its duty, paperwork written, signed sealed delivered.

Back on the street, I make my way to the gated inspection center,
keeping visible, not to alarm guards but as I enter the yard, a man
shouts Stop! Which I do, spread my arms. *You can't come in.*

I just want to know what the dog is for. He shakes his head. *Just go.*
And I do, but as I turn the corner he's talking to another guard,
who starts in my direction. A question, I shout. He comes closer.

What's going on with that yellow dog? He shrugs, confused.
We check everything that comes in, you know. I don't know, I say.
He studies me. I study him, his pressed uniform, missing a tooth.

Tell me, I confide, *does that yellow dog ever find anything?*
He pauses, thinking what to say. *Thank God,* he replies. *No.* Which
is how I discovered New York City's secret surveillance society.

Coming Clean

We knew each other as rude kids
in high school but hadn't been together
for decades when we meet
at an old watering hole on 54th Street.
He doesn't look very different,
except in the hair department
and a big chest that suggests serious
physical activity or steroids.
I'm clean, he says, hinting about what
he'd been doing in Los Angeles.
He reads the menu carefully, saying
he'd come into money and orders
single malt Scotch for us both.
He tells me stories of body-building,
making a film about a boxer
that never got finished, sounding
a bit like brag or baloney.
He keeps the whiskey coming,
talking sometimes as if I'm not there
but he's watching my reactions.
I can tell he is getting around
to something. *Quite a life,*
I finally interrupt, and he stops,
startled. I ask if he has anyone
he talks to. *Sure,* he says. *You.*
It takes a while. He digresses
to Chicago, a motel near the airport,
up a flight of stairs, handing over a bag
of cash, getting nothing back.
The guy ran, he fired a shot, killed him.
That's the punch line. I say nothing.
He pays the bill with plastic.
We agree we won't wait
another twenty years. And we don't.
At 6 AM, my phone rings.
You remember that story?
Is that a question?
I made it up. It was the whiskey.
Whatever you say, I reply,
suddenly aware I've become
the man who knew too much.

Almost Sullen

He was quiet, almost sullen. Four years
in the Navy taught him good posture,
a prudent fear of authority
easily mistaken for kissing ass.

Many days we shared a lunch hour
in the library basement, held ardent talks
about our work-in-progress. Caution
was his byword, anxiety his spur.

His career thrived—teacher, author, TV
pundit. A modest man, he didn't stay
in touch. Then gossip rose: his wife left,
took custody of the child. He lived alone.

We met once by chance, he showed a spiritual
side—zen, yoga, an interest in sacred hymns.
He lost the mid-life paunch, grew a white beard,
exuded gravitas, wisdom, equanimity.

He surprised me, last we spoke, divulged
sadness never visible—abandoned by both
parents: one drunk, one too poor to keep him.
How well I knew him—and not at all.

PART 4

Miracles on 23RD Street (Before the Cell Phone)

The telephone, the dial, the receiver,
the phone booth, the coin: His name

is Mickenberg, listed in the Manhattan
Directory, but where is the phone book?

On 23rd Street, hottest day of the year
I look for a phone book in a phone booth.

Every corner seems to have one, except
at the first one, the cord is cut, book gone.

Ditto the next booth, ditto the one after that.
I cool off in a diner, ask the man for the book.

We don't have one, he says. *Someone took it.*
Ditto at the deli, the haberdasher, the bank.

It's a long, long thirsty walk until I see a library
ahead, sure it has the book, but today it's closed.

I pause outside the YMCA, rest against the cool
facade. Eyes shut, open, shut, open: I glimpse

a mirage, a complete Manhattan phone book lies
at my feet. I lift the miracle gift, find the number,

rush to the booth under the stairs at the Chelsea Hotel.
I put in a quarter, get the dial tone, listen to the ring.

And the ring the ring the ring ringing. No answer.
I bang the receiver back on the hook—Goodbye

Mister Mickenberg—and out splashes a jangle of coins,
quarters spilling from the box—at last, the lottery!

Shopping on 34TH Street

It's hard to put your arm around
the Empire State Building for a selfie
but the lobby has a mock-up to scale.

A wet Monday morning I lend my aid
so tourists can take blurry family shots
to prove they've seen the elephant.

They are grateful for assistance, especially
out-of-town Americans who chat about
the lovely towns they've left behind.

Travel, for them, is a form of shopping,
really the only reason for taking vacations
they say, to find bargains and logos galore.

As for photos, serious buffs stay blocks
away, align cameras to snap happy faces
posed under King Kong's long spire.

That's realism. The lens catches full
plumage nearby—not still billboards
of Cadillac cars or snarling blonde stars.

Now giant screens show athletes in brand
names, makeup artists applying skin cream,
models in bikinis, couples basking in sunlight.

These ads embrace America's sacred holidays:
Go Shopping, exercise your rights as consumers.
I mean, what else is the point of President's Day?

Not Talking to Strangers

Waiting for the light to change
outside Pennsylvania station
one autumn Saturday afternoon

I overhear someone mumble
Are you white?
realize he's talking to me.

The young man who asks
is not (I think) and cringing
I refuse to answer,

watch him move on to
someone else. Leaving me
to wonder how white am I?

Are Jews (like me) or Irish
or Mediterranean Catholics
really white as WASPs?

I'm that and not that,
reject both the honor
and the yellow star.

Not likely that's why the young
stranger asked the question. Would
the distinction matter?

Who you think I am
I should have said
is who I know I'm not.

Making Peace

Coming toward me, a young black man,
wool cap angled, refuses to meet my eye.
White skin will not—cannot—intimidate
his step. When I mumble *Good Mornin'*
he breaks into smiles but keeps on going
and so do I.

In my blood, no slave owners, no traders,
none wore rebel gray nor imagined holding
a whip or chain. My white Dad boasted
of riding around the Delta at the back of
the buses from Memphis to Biloxi.
We picketed Woolworth's, marched
for open housing, spoke out.

What recompense do we owe for evil
done by others—our own conscience clear—
when not to do something lets it seem
as if nothing terrible happened? But it has.
Someday, mister, we'll stop, shake hands.

Harry

For years I've been trying to get a bead on
my friend Harry, the painter, and yesterday
he dropped by to repair a fallen valence,
for which I complimented his adroitness
and he responded by saying he was good
at dropping things, including dropping out
of high school to join the white panther
branch of the Black Panther party just as
the FBI was arresting Black kids by
the dozens. Harry's first task was
to drive four Black women to visit
their incarcerated men at an out-of-town
prison. He picked them up at dawn
as they were leaving an all-night
lingerie party. The women settled down,
passing joints for breakfast, teasing
with Harry, the butt of humor about panties,
stockings, and bras until they arrived
near the gates, and the women
had to remove their street clothing
in the car to re-dress in proper Muslim
attire for their husbands and boyfriends.
Harry enjoyed their company
and when they returned home
they invited him to a family-style
spaghetti feed, where Harry shared
garlic bread with many future
Black Power leaders. They liked
him, he liked them, but after that great
meal he knew his job had no future.

Fight or Flight

I'm sitting in a noisy midtown bar,
my buddy Bruce, part-time detective
surveilling a woman wearing blue

as he describes the newest snooping
devices he uses to eavesdrop, certain
parties doing things they shouldn't,

when the volume at the next table rises,
two large men on their feet, fists flying,
dragging themselves out the door.

I'm content to admire the scuffle from
a distance, two drunks, probably someone
lost a bet or insulted the blue woman

but before I register what's happening
Bruce has leaped from his chair, races
out to witness the street fight unfold.

Crime and punishment, I think, he's
doing his business, but quickly Bruce
steps between the fighters and they stop.

Until then, I couldn't imagine risking blood
to bust up a brawl, caution I was born with,
but what he did gives me a fresh idea.

Not enough to witness. Some things need
to be stopped. I see Bruce outside calming
the fighters as the crowd slowly disperses.

I decide to step in, talk to the blue woman,
tell her it's time. Before he comes back. Go.
Get out. Now, and she runs for the back door.

Fugitive

Around Grand Central Station, Sunday morning, homeless men
snuggle in doorways, sleeping off Saturday night, avoiding people

except for a certain shirtless man, his chest blotched with scars,
striding fast, his look anxious. Behind him two police officers,

man, woman in pursuit, not quite running, follow him through
the maze of travelers, see him slip out an exit and disappear.

The cops slow down, the woman raises one palm, giving a hand
gesture that translates *Good riddance.* They stand still

for a long moment, making sure the runaway doesn't return.
He escaped, I speak to the cop. *Yeah,* she says, *So what?*

The Broadcast

Trying some modest exercise, I follow green lights
and foot traffic until the sun peeps on a hillside above
Hudson's river, soft mist dripping off oak and maple.

The grounds nearly empty except for a morning drunk
wearing cowboy boots, orange turtleneck, stretched on
a bench, talking aloud through a coiled cardboard sheet

resembling a megaphone, making vulgar comments to
strolling passersby, most attending to dogs, but now
addressed to a lady wearing a black cape, open at the neck,

revealing jewels of consequence. She's leading a white terrier
that unfortunately stops in front of the announcer, who begins
to imitate a high-pitched sports reporter marveling at a scene

as the little pup hunches his back to shit, the spiel describing
exactly what's happening before his eyes: *There he is...he is
squatting, squeezing a bit. Yes, and out comes the first poop...*

and another...and now he's standing up...and his mistress—
her face a mix of smirk and shame—*is bending, yes bending
over and look ...she's got a plastic baggie...and she's stooping*

*to pick up the poops...ah yes, and she's a little shy, but every
dog has his day and today the mutt is a star*—the distraught lady
clutches in one hand the leather leash and between her thumb

and forefinger holds tight to the little bag like a teacup and gets
the hell out of there as fast as she can. *There she goes,* he says.
I get the hell out too, before the idiot gets the goods on me.

Anonymous City

A day before Thanksgiving, wind bitter,
everyone hurrying towards any indoors,

all we want is warmth, except for an elder
woman in a wool cap in Harlem hovering
with a homeless person hiding from weather
under cardboard on the sidewalk.

It's not your fault, I overhear her say,
it's the system.

Freezing slowly, I seek a pit stop that isn't
a franchise. None here, forces me to deploy
into a familiar brand that won't require
a purchase to pee. I sit opposite a student
eating a western omelet with a plastic fork,
eyes on her screen. She never knew I was there.

The anonymous city, yes, but also an intimate
haven, even the fast food chains—each separate,
each the same—show local ambiance, workers
doing their jobs: one turns the salads, one draws
coffee, one mops, a manager handles the cash.

Not to be confused with friendship, shared hours
of labor. I hear two wait persons sniping at a boss,
private intimacy that comes with the job, but won't
last. When someone's let go or quits, it's all over.

Forever. They'll never meet again.

PART 5

The Americans

"The last Thursday in November...is the one day
that is purely American." —Sydney Porter (O'Henry)

After the turkey's been sliced and eaten, my thoughts
turn to past Thanksgivings, hosting our open house,
the old folks gone, reading O'Henry aloud to the kids,

but now as adults they propose another postprandial
binge, beyond boring pumpkin pie, to watch a TV series
aptly named *The Americans* about Russian spies,

"a true story," so they say, about a handsome couple
raising a typical suburban family as they seduce
clueless citizens and ferret government secrets.

Aliens by birth and training, the characters adjust easily
to indigenous lifestyles—pizza, Coke, TV and hang out
over beers with their close neighbor, an FBI spy catcher.

Their parallel lives blur, as their children have crushes,
the real Americans divorce, and the fakers stick as true
lovers committed to the cold warrior code of violence.

Tending to home fires, the spooks conduct their crimes
with shameless guile—wear shades, wigs, beards, and lie
to all, and reveal a subtle expertise in killing their foes.

On this purely American day, nonetheless, I'm rooting for
the enemy, as the filmmakers apparently intend. Compared
to the counter-spies, the Ruskies treat each other kindly.

The liberated mother shares equally the thrill and danger
of fighting against a country run by dull men and grooms
her daughter in the fine arts of karate and espionage.

Even when trapped, our fugitives escape as smoothly as
Houdini slipped lock and chain. They are *me* in my wildest
fantasy of freedom, beating Big Brother and the gods of law.

Immigrants

Captured in the photo, they cluster
as strangers, no one I would know
but for notes my mother scribbled.
The girl in glasses was her sister Bertie,
who on a day off work went ice skating,
fell backwards, died sleeping next
to my mother who kept the night alive.

Clutching a stuffed lamb, my mother
is almost out of the picture, her brother
Louis wears the same goofy grin I saw
when he told jokes or lies. The elders
pose like salt & pepper shakers, young,
hardly the old folks I saw grow frail.

Behind the stiff faces sit two ancient people—
him with a square beard, her a prayer shawl—
my great-grandparents, greenhorns brought
by their children to the promised land.

Here the future begins again, half my DNA
carrying hope and courage that led them
across borders, gunshots in the night,
an entire ocean to America, where after
years of labor they rest in unvisited graves.

Nearly anonymous in life, so they remain.
They struggled to live for as long as
they could, though with these few words from
my mother's stories, maybe a moment longer.

Borscht

My grandpa Izzy adored borscht, slurped
the soup, steaming or cold, let the red juice
spread on his mustache and licked his lips.

Borscht. A Russian scholar once advised me
never to underestimate its power to make
a community, and in honor of Izzy I bought

the scholar's book about early factory workers
in Tsarist Russia, depicting the daily lives
of a struggling people unknown to history.

They might be characters of literature, people
inhabiting the worlds of Tolstoy, Turgenev,
Dostoyevsky, yet are not fictional, revealing

dreams of ordinary men and women seeking
fair working conditions in a new industrial age.
As a class, they drink too much, eat too little,

are sent to prison for their trouble. The author
shows harsh conditions of work under foremen
who demand payment or sex from women workers,

and the failure of students who propose reforms
from books the workers can't understand. Yet
he offers something they never expected, maybe

even more than the author imagined. He's given
these Russians historical immortality, while
revealing how limited were Izzy's opportunities,

a working-class Jew, lacking even the slim benefits
of Russian nationality. Refusing the harsh discipline
of factory work, he became an itinerant glazier,

carried his tools on his back, worked outdoors without
a timeclock in all weather; and he loved the glass he cut
because of all the light, he said, it brought to life.

A Wound in the Heart

I

Mayday, the earth warms, greens, a trumpet on the car radio
bleeds, Miles Davis, *Sketches of Spain,* the drama of rebirth,
a staccato horn chases the bull in an arena, cycles of disorder.

Here comes the matador, here comes the bull dripping blood
from black shoulder muscle, the red cape hiding the silver sword,
minor keys whipping the animal agony, driving to the fated end.

It was in Spain in the Seventies I first saw the face of fascism,
the Guardia Civil walking in pairs, armed with black pistols,
submachine guns, also in the faces of hotel clerks demanding

passports, holding them for days, just in case…. Forty years fear
under Generalissimo Franco, ally of Mussolini and Hitler, who
bombed Guernica, and beat the elected Republic to a pulp.

I knew little about Spain's Civil War. My father had showed me
a spiral-bound book of pastel drawings, Republican soldiers in arms.
He had friends who fought in the International Brigades, the famed

Lincoln battalion, and he refused to visit Spain while the dictator lived,
but he understood and forgave why I would go there to meet a woman.
Under a blazing sun, the brass blares, the taunted bull falls to its knees.

2

Spain nestles inside, its tragedy my passion. I collect stories of war,
spoken history of veterans, and now in the 1990s I'm walking streets
in Moscow, or searching in long-lost archives of the Spanish war.

I've asked my translator, Galina, what she wanted from America. *Jazz,*
she says and I bring her a rare vinyl of *Sketches,* but when I get there,
she admits what she really wants is a Big Mac at Moscow's McDonald's.

What has brought the collapse of the Soviet empire lingers in open air—
massive potholes in sidewalks, broken windows and stairwells, two-hour
queues to buy black bread, gas leaks, polluted water, drunks everywhere.

Near Red Square you can watch a steady parade, brides, grooms, kneeling
at an eternal flame for the anti-fascist dead. I'm carrying letters for two
Spanish war veterans who will speak about death in the olive groves.

3

Morris Cohen, Bronx-born (my native land) fought with guerrillas
in Spain, learned tricks of the trade for his life's work in espionage.
An old *brigadista* hinted at Cohen's story, warned me to be careful.

In the heat of the Cold War, FBI ferreting atom bomb spies, Morris
and his wife abruptly disappear from New York. No one knows why,
but when agents break a Red spy ring they find photos of Cohen.

Just as I'm about to fly to Russia, out of the blue I receive a letter
asking me to visit Cohen at a Moscow address. Scary but exciting.
It takes Galina a couple of weeks to muster nerve to accompany me.

I ring the doorbell of a brick building on a quiet, tree-lined street,
out steps a soldier with a weapon strapped to his back, invites us in.
We have found headquarters of Russian intelligence. Galina's face

drains all color. I show my letter from Cohen, the soldier stomps
upstairs, returns with Boris, who looks me over and promises a reply.
I hadn't told him where I'm living. Already he knows how to find me.

4

While I wait for his call, I track down another veteran, Percy Ludwig,
tall, gaunt, expert in building fortifications in Spain. Raised in London,
he speaks Cockney, his family Jewish Socialists deported back to Russia.

Percy lives in a huge building, a Brezhnev blockhouse, he quips,
poorly furnished rooms, floors creaky. His wife serves plates of bony fish.
Framed photos show them working artillery during the big war.

They were teachers when Stalin went on an anti-Jew campaign, Percy lost
his job. Now in their eighties, they live in poverty, another side
of Soviet failure. As I leave that night, he flashes his fist in a radical salute.

5

Russian intelligence calls, Boris will take me to Morris Cohen,
resting in a military hospital, late stages of heart failure.
Galina tags along, seriously impressed by my first-class contacts.

In bed, legs swollen, his mind lucid, he asks about old comrades,
talks of a happy childhood in the Bronx, football at Monroe High
and Mississippi, names a friend killed down South for civil rights.

I bring the conversation to Spain, his guerrilla work, setting bombs,
ciphering radio codes. His voice is didactic. In fact, he never stops
talking, as if starved for intimacy in his native language.

I take a chance, hope Boris won't intervene, ask Morris if he regrets
his life of spying. It was unthinkable, he replies, for one country to
have a monopoly of such terrible weapons. All I want is peace.

6

Spain, where anti-fascist resistance started, moves to democracy,
honors the International Brigades that faced fascism before it was
fashionable. In the US, they were tagged *premature anti-fascists*.

Call it history. All these years later, what could have been different:
If democracies stopped fascism in Spain, would Hitler have run ahead?
Would there even have been a race to make atom bombs?

At a veterans reunion, troubled by tragedy that might have been avoided,
I notice a woman looking Russian sitting alone. Percy Ludwig? I ask.
She shakes her head, tells me after his wife died, he jumped out a window.

The fascists won that war, but the losers had better poetry. Albert Camus
said defeat was a wound in the heart ... *that one can be right and yet
be vanquished, that force can subdue the spirit.*

Grace

Years ago we met on cobblestones
in Madrid. I was footloose, thirsty,
looking for trouble when she crossed
into my path, her heel grinding
hard, set me afire from toe to teeth.

She's all woman, in my mind,
I call her Grace, the way she enters
my room when I least expect her,
radiant but pungent, assertive,
consuming, subtle, destructive.

I hobbled and grit for weeks,
forced to quit my itinerary,
settling for sedentary tourism.
No walking to sightsee, no standing
in lines at the Sofia, the Prado.

I rented a rowboat to feel my body
float, mostly I sat in cafes studying
the soul of Spanish pleasure, slow
taste of tapas, interminable sips
of latte or the bite of aquavit.

How much more I saw than stations
of the cross. Sun bleaching out pain,
the pause seemed a blessing. Almost
I wanted to thank that woman
who I never expected to see again.

Years later in Los Angeles, at a party
of writers and publishers, whiskey
flowing, I tangled feet dancing with
a lady I didn't recognize, until
suddenly realizing a familiar agony.

My body whimpered all the way home,
The handyman working in my studio
took a look, gave the diagnosis: drinking
too much, too much testosterone, casual
encounters, dehydration—GOUT!

When I was young her stealth prompted
ridicule, as if her tortures fit my crimes.
Lately, I get only pity—a lonely old man
playing with matches but she never fails,
attacks when called, fills my cup with grief.

PART 6

Fresh Meadows

Even the tacky suburbs mature. I picture
our landlords Bill & Betty who lived in
a basement flat below our apartment, not
ashamed to beg for advances on the rent.

Always broke, they were notorious drunks
on Saturday nights, but Sunday mornings
became holy, took their boy in a white shirt
to worship, subscribed to the Watchtower.

Taught to be polite, Steve never swore
but once when no one was around, led me
into Uncle Hugh's closet to open a deck
of French playing cards, 52 sexual poses!

I can see Betty in a pink slip perspiring
over the ironing board, Bill washing
a dinky Ford, hosing down his tomatoes.
Poor as church mice, my mother sighed.

Recently, I passed the old house wearing
a fresh yellow coat, the ratty barn gone,
fruit trees prospering, the soil surely risen
in worth, whoever lives there now is rich.

The Philanthropist

He built a fortune, tens of millions, never mind
how, mostly investments—and then began to give
away his money, paying back in spades,
as he put it, the capitalist system that starved
his immigrant family in the east Bronx.

Though he knew their needs, he seldom
gave cash to charities, instead embraced
a near-extinct species—call them activists
or radicals or agitators—plain people who
struggled for justice, picketing with strikers,
fighting city hall, whistle blowers and
media informing about abuses of power.

He proved as good at giving as at making.

He would not be seduced by zealots bragging
of rebellion nor tempted by unlikely dreamers,
but preferred steady quiet resistance—educating
the public, keeping a democratic faith to make
life safer, fair, some faraway day.

He's 90, his body weak, I take the moment
to applaud his vision. He responds, thanking
me for something I barely remember saying
(the throwaway a poet offers a philanthropist)
nothing is more valuable than giving love.

He looks through teary eyes. Loving, he says;
making money was much easier than loving.
He blushes, finding something so late in life.
Taking love is hard too, he adds, eyes brimming
at what he doesn't do well, can't quite accept.

Wall Street, Occupied

Sprawled on a sun-bleached sidewalk, the teachers
scribble red ink down the margins of homework,
a holiday weekend, they are pleading for their jobs.
1984 IS NOT AN INSTRUCTIONAL MANUAL!

This is Wall Street occupied by maniacs who haven't
yet abandoned love for the young: the algebra expert
reassigned by her principal to teach pre-kindergarten
so she'll quit, be replaced by a lower-paid teacher.

Someone starts drumming a bongo, a familiar tune rises,
yes, and a hundred voices lift the melody, humming
through the unsingable parts of the lyrical war cry
to the land of the free—repeat, land of the free—FREE!

Even patrolman Miele, armed with baton, pistol, whistle,
worries that youth will run amok through Liberty Square,
but reveals a personal, tentative smile at the outlaws
who terrify politicians with our national anthem.

Wall Street, home of America's fictional corporate individual
claiming constitutional rights to buy politics, is no random target.
The only words these corporations know, says a news reporter,
is more. A woman's placard announces GREED KILLS...

Ghosts of the Great Depression—gray men grimacing
on soup lines, bread winners no longer bringing home
the bacon, forfeiting the love of their wives, young
women hoisting skirts over their knees for a nickel.

Not here, not now, not despairing, not yet, but hopeful,
extravagantly expectant. Naïve, I hear the cynics chant,
foolish, idealistic, child-like dreamers—all true, of course.
They sing, coming at last to the climax, *home of the brave.*

Imaginary Characters

The richest persons never go on diets,
never binge, they're pure No-bodies,
imaginary characters like Donald Duck's
Uncle Scrooge, the Disney cheapskate
who quacks with joy when swimming
in pools of dimes and dollar bills.

Hard to picture a make-believe citizen,
ghost-like, extending invisible hands,
red tooth and claw—and despite
lack of vocal cords or cranium—
expressing opinions
in forms of cold cash and credit.

That state of mind most sympathetic
to corporate fantasies considers
its Boards families, passing
a legacy, culture, assets, health and wealth
through preferred stocks and bonds.

Speak no evil of their immense worth —
they mean well, they say—and pay
no attention to profits drawn from
spills and poisons that live on earth forever.

Do not envy these ethereal persons, clever
as angels and who, like them, shall never die.
Remember (as the great McGuffey put it)
the rich have many troubles which we know nothing of.

Class Reunion

Searching Google for an old soldier,
I land on the wrong man
but listed one name above
someone I've not seen for fifty years,

the brilliant girl in the next seat,
Seventh Grade English,
the most likely to succeed
and there's her blue-lettered email.

We meet a month later in a white linen café,
she brings another friend from our class.
We look at each other—our eyes
cannot pause.

How it began, in the heat
of adolescent ambition; here now,
almost at the end, admiring
our yellow-fin tuna with ginger.

Once we were promising scholars
at Mr. Parsons Junior High—
the orchestra class, each a potential
musician or perhaps an engineer.

Now we're twice as old
as our parents were then.
Beneath wrinkles,
splotches, white hair,
an old scar slowly shows.

A familiar voice asks
where was it we ate hotdogs
for 15 cents?—as if the answer,
The Lucky Seven,
gives a password to the past.

Your mother? someone starts
—oh, I'm so sorry;
a person gone for six or 30 years
the sorrow no less sincere.

We seem to like ourselves,
though I detect slight rivalry
or jealousy, not about success
but our vulnerability, hoping
to be well remembered.

I want most to say
I'm sorry for the boy
I must have been.
Don't bother, someone replies,
no one really cares
any more.

Of thirty in the class,
few could not be found;
three were dead and one more since.
Some were widowed, many
more divorced. All are white,

puzzled by those who stay away
by choice or chance.
Maybe shame.
Luck is the wild card.

As amazing, the ease of discovery,
finding these strangers. No one
can hide forever, no one's anonymous,
and we still expect to grow up.

Look Me Up

Girls were a step ahead, knew a thing or two
about art, theater, Emily Dickinson,
in some primal way understood what power
their bodies held, or soon would.

The tall redhead, large boned, lightly
colored lips shaped into a smirk,
her voice smoky, hummed to herself—
adored Elvis, his Heartbreak Hotel.

At 13, she waved goodbye in my slam book:
When you are about 25, look me up/it will be
interesting both ways. . .love and stuff.
p.s. it's been nice—as if I knew what she meant.

When I turned 25, married with child,
a Minneapolis homeowner with bright red
sideburns and mustache, a penchant for weed,
I didn't even think of her, though now I know:

Hanging out with jazz fiends, she picked up a taste
for speed and smack, a classmate saw her once
in the middle of a Manhattan street shouting
at an African man (not the right moment to say hi).

She wasn't easy to find after that, until I saw
a magazine story about an AIDS hospice—
red-haired ex-coke addict/prostitute driven by disease
to dry out, admitting she'd been a lousy hooker.

I'm a product of a progressive education, she brags,
but has lost her sense of balance, uses a wheelchair—
I've had this disease so long, she admits. *I'm tired*—
the first of us to ride the dark side of the lonely street.

The Table

Three of us sitting in a small office in Manhattan,
knees and ankles colliding with every move, the two
women each shy of 50 and me, milestones ahead,
when one of these mid-life beauties suggests, gently
of course, that I might be over-the-hill more ways
than the body knows, out of touch with the times.

Startled, unable to object, I feel reality descend,
not for lack of defense but dead true. Age makes me quaint.
No rudeness intended, none taken, a social fact—
yes, but the strength of memory remains, knowing more
merely more—gives a person a claim at this shaky table,
where I'm still irreplaceable for now.

Winter Solstice

The grand piano rests on roller skates
in the middle of Washington Square,
a stenciled motto over the keyboard

THIS MACHINE KILLS FASCISTS

the bearded pianist removes mittens,
surveys the stragglers who fall quiet,
pounds the first chord of *Nocturne*

scaring a small flock of city pigeons
into the frigid sky, stirring a moment
of awe, as the melody continues, sweet

calm of a Sunday morning in the park.
I drop two bills into the gift bowl, honor
to Woody Guthrie's anti-fascist slogan.

Under a weak sun, the West Village stays
quaint and quiet, high school kids lining
outside Joe's Pizza, as they always have.

A man on a bench tries to feed ice cream to
a confused pigeon. Someone's hand-painted
PLEASE VOTE near a Rat Poison warning.

Around the corner a puffy bundled lady
sells holiday wreathes that hang above
a hand-lettered sign from the zodiac.

     Is the sun afraid to die?

The Blizzard

I was a one-night visitor until weather struck my plans,
forced to face the storm in a West Village high-rise.
Stopping to stock up, I find an unshaved half-naked
man, elbows on the sidewalk, watching me closely.

Wind begins to bite, the sky turns smoky gray, a tarp
on the balcony slaps the window. Flurries fill the air,
queer journey swept by crosswinds, sticking to squares
of dirt that root city trees, settle in concrete cracks.

At dusk, the wind slows, white stuff thickens, sweeps
streets, covers parked cars, the wind churning patterns
of white spires high as a cathedral, until it reverses,
de-spirals, then upsweeps to form fresh-spired towers.

Hour by hour white descends, intensifying silence indoors.
Suddenly, for no particular reason, my host says *We're safe.*
I immerse myself in books, aware of raw soundlessness
more powerful than gypsy songs playing in the next room.

One night and a day before the sky calms. Midnight in
wool and boots we explore graceful drifts, curved as
human limbs, amber lamps painting snow. Briefly,
the wind rises, an icy crust tumbles on my bare head.

How brief the pause. A dawn siren breaks sleep, my heart
stirring to emergency. I trudge through slush to the grocery,
its threshold carpeted by flattened boxes whereon sits
that unshaved man who survived, watching me closely.

Snow Day

Sunbreak in the city, snow
half melted, refrozen, crunchy
in a glove, watching a shaved-scalp man
chase a screaming girl in a parking lot,
he throws, hits the heel of her boot
as she turns fast to face him.

A history of snow freezes my head,
I know a thing or two about the white
chill, being shoved into a drift,
face washed on a sub-zero day.

Now the girl counterattacks, lobs
a chunk of winter, the arc wild, ice
hits my neck, arouses an instinct
to avenge, but shock crosses her face.

Sorry, mister, first snow, I'm a little crazy.
Me too, and I'm a little too old to fight.

Unreliable Narrator

Distant rumors of fear, a crime
attributed to the stony-faced leader
denying the doctor's warning,
even after the doctor died.

Numbers leak through
subterranean pipelines, hearsay,
as paranoids issue warnings
the sober, the sane, the faraway
choose to overlook.

Suddenly, cancel everything,
even the funeral of one who died
of natural causes. Save your
words for another epitaph.

I make a pot of spaghetti,
big enough for two leftover meals
and think again
of the blizzard, New York 2016

when in the shelter of great silence
my friend called out
We're safe
and I could believe him.

Through a Dark Window

Where I always sit, a table for two
alone, looking out the Tick Tock's
cloudy window toward Penn station,

across the street a squad of grimy men,
dozing on the sidewalk, backs to a brick wall,
a food cart under a yellow umbrella

at the curb, the smell of fried oil
or maybe the warmth of steaming pots
attract the hungry and the homeless.

Inside my nook, Michael the Ukrainian waiter
brings a bowl of noodle soup,
a grilled cheese sandwich, one pickle,

and fifteen minutes of ease. He cracks
a joke, I show approval, and each of us—
Michael, the busy cook, those lonely

and lost outside—try to live as best we can,
some version of being happy
in this weary time of a late winter day.

Spring weeks away will bring me back
to the Tick Tock, though rumors fly
like snowflakes, tumble sideways

as the wind shifts. Something else
seems to be blowing into the big city
from who knows where—China? Italy?

Is it too late to go home?
Something ominous, unpredictable.
What to do? Where to stay?

PART 7

Memory as Hope

After what you've gone through,
says the surgeon. *I'll give you
six-point-five.* Years, he adds.

How little they know,
how much I desire:
facts, stats, decimals.

After that, eyes twinkling,
he shows a sliver of irony.
You will want six-point-five more.

Who exactly is this You
he addresses? Not Mister Before.
Forever you're Mister After.

I take six-point-five in doses,
by days I mean, one by one
then another. That way

I never forget a day, nor try to
predict. I've become particular
about my dose: Sunrise, please.

I embark on local wanderings,
one day come upon an immigrant-
looking man planting four saplings.

My unpainterly eye opens to color,
everything not linen-white overflows,
I see eloquence in his Jacaranda.

He spreads water from a blue pail,
attaches chartreuse stakes to a limb,
violet blossoms sparkle in sunlight.

I interrupt to praise his labor,
he smiles like a sly detective, looking
into the ungrateful heavens.

I'm not the poet of gardens, plants,
flowers, but trees hold history like people.
One must be optimistic to root trees.

Six-point-five known, my unit of time,
no desire to leave work undone,
I abandon all long-term projects.

Meaning no more meetings with agents,
editors, publicists. Meaning Allan Ginsberg's
archive, 1,400 linear feet, I will not read.

As wound heals to scar, each twinge
focuses interest on what's failing
inside, organic narcissism I resist.

I become fascinated by missing persons,
go in search of former classmates,
and long ago lost lovers, dead relatives.

A brown photo of my mother's family—she's
two, holding a stuffed lamb—makes me wonder
which of my remains will puzzle my heirs.

Scraps of thwarted stories, the unfinished novel:
my impulse is to destroy evidence, though
not as meticulously as old tax receipts.

Strange that novel returns, so many run-on
sentences signaling how the frenzied brain
couldn't hold the excitement of my mind.

I name the hero General America, who refuses
to obey the rules of capitalism, such as paying
fees for bounced checks or interest on loans.

He embodies my anarchist dream to ignite
disorder, disrespect for uniforms, weddings,
pledges of allegiance at sporting events.

Now time kills my enthusiasm for make-believe.
I abandon work-in-progress, put pages in a box,
still can't decide whether to burn the box.

I gain time to watch the backyard redwood tree
grow taller each rainy season, though it's hard
to measure annual increase while the tree lives.

The straight spine suggests majesty, serenity even
when winter winds agitate high branches. I notice
black squirrels kneeling like priests at its roots.

My front yard looks like wind-blown magic,
a drooping willow, sinewy limbs intricate as
a ballerina's skeleton stretching into Pacific mist.

Volunteer seeds, what birds bring in their bowels,
populate what was once a garden, my wilderness
of dark-brown bark, a shelter and a hiding place.

In the house, under ceiling skylights, the woman
I live with guides me on a tour of the rooms, shows
me the bed I missed while my transplants set.

I start over, six point five sweeter than zeroes,
living my days in time without contagious anger.
I notice nothing important in the world is about me.

Our New Century

Computers predicted the gridlock,
a virus (Y2K) would force airplanes
to fall from the sky, bank accounts
to empty themselves, passwords
to disappear, credit cards would expire.

No one wanted to start over in 1900
though no one could explain why not,
as if the twentieth century was bad
enough already, and no one had learned
a single lesson to avert its return.

Gridlock soon tied the presidential election
when ballots disintegrated into thin air
or drooped like corpses called hanging chads.
One court overruled another until
it was *Hail to the Chief* 5-4.

The lucky president, unfairly accused
of dyslexia, was lucidly reading a storybook
(*The Runaway Bunny*) to a kindergarten class
when the evil ones robbed four jet planes
killing thousands. Naturally he had to retaliate.

Politicians don't talk of modern art, even
Picasso's *Guernika* showing bombings
by Nazi warplanes. A copy hangs in the UN,
in the very room the US ambassador asks
for permission to bomb Iraq.

What would the world think? I know what
I think, so the ambassador made sure to draw
a curtain over the painting and no one
would see it. Then everyone was on
the cake-walk to Baghdad.

Next came a hurricane that drowned New Orleans.
Next came a hurricane that drowned New York.
Next came a hurricane that drowned Texas.
Next came a wildfire that parched California.
No one needed a weatherman to know anything.

Even a person of color could be elected president.
Next a white vigilante killed Trevor Martin, 17.
Next a white Missouri cop shot Michael Brown, 18.
Next a white Cleveland cop shot Tamir Rice, 12
Next, etc. etc. etc. etc. etc. etc. etc. etc. etc. etc. etc

When the bankers realized mortgage bonds
were worthless, where could they turn for
help but the White House, the Fed, and
the bones of their debtors who should
have known better and read the fine print.

A Supreme Court with appropriate gravity
reminded people that corporations actually
were imaginary citizens who could live like
angels, forever, and had the same rights
to give money to politicians as real citizens.

Sometimes the Court showed it could
laugh. When some cities claimed that
citizens did not need to own machine guns,
the judges said *ha, ha, ha,* and sent thoughts
and prayers to all dead school children.

And still the charmed republic stands
as a haven, thousands flock to its borders,
clinging to rags and empty water bottles.
Many were quickly arrested, kids tossed
into cages, parents hanging on to hope.

When all is not lost, a real virus arrives,
more gridlock, masks versus freedom,
quarantines versus business. Which is more
important? You already know whose
lives don't matter as much as other lives.

When unemployment gets too high to support
people's lives, guess what? Washington goes
into gridlock, and it's only twenty years since
the new century brought happiness. *Thank you,*
our leaders like to say. *God bless America.*

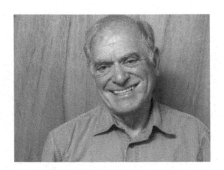

About the Author

Talking to Strangers, Peter Neil Carroll's seventh volume of poetry, unravels stories and sensibilities of everyday life for and about ordinary people. His previous collections include *Fracking Dakota: Poems for a Wounded Land* (Turning Point, 2015); *The Truth Lies on Earth* (Turning Point, 2018) as well as *An Elegy for Lovers; Something is Bound to Break;* and *A Child Turns Back to Wave: Poetry of Lost Places* which won the Prize Americana from the Institute for the Study of American Popular Culture. An earlier volume, *Riverborne: A Mississippi Requiem,* explores the lonely world of America's great river. His poems have appeared in many journals and online publications. He has published over twenty books, including the memoir, *Keeping Time.* He has taught creative writing at the University of San Francisco, taught history and American Studies at Stanford and Berkeley, hosted "Booktalk" on Pacifica Radio, and edited the San Francisco Review of Books. He is currently Poetry Moderator of Portside.org and lives in northern California with the writer/photographer Jeannette Ferrary.

Also By Peter Neil Carroll

POETRY

Something Is Bound To Break
An Elegy For Lovers
The Truth Lies On Earth: A Year By Dark, By Bright
Fracking Dakota: Poems For A Wounded Land
A Child Turns Back To Wave: Poetry Of Lost Places
Riverborne: A Mississippi Requiem

NON-FICTION (SELECTED)

Keeping Time: Memory, Nostalgia & The Art of History
The Odyssey of The Abraham Lincoln Brigade: Americans
        in The Spanish Civil War
From Guernica to Human Rights: Essays on The Spanish Civil War
It Seemed Like Nothing Happened: America in The 1970s
The Free & The Unfree: A New History (With David W. Noble)
Puritanism & The Wilderness